The Story Of SAVANT
Told using Automatic Drawings and
Surreal Art written in the style of
Scholars' Art

Camilia MacPherson, Ph.D., D.Th.

INTRODUCTION
This book is written using Scholars' Art. That is,
automatic drawings and surreal art are used to convey
meaning. These pages are written in consecutive order.
Each page has to be looked at from every angle and
varying distances. There is no top or bottom of the page.
In every page there is a surplus of meaning with several
images.

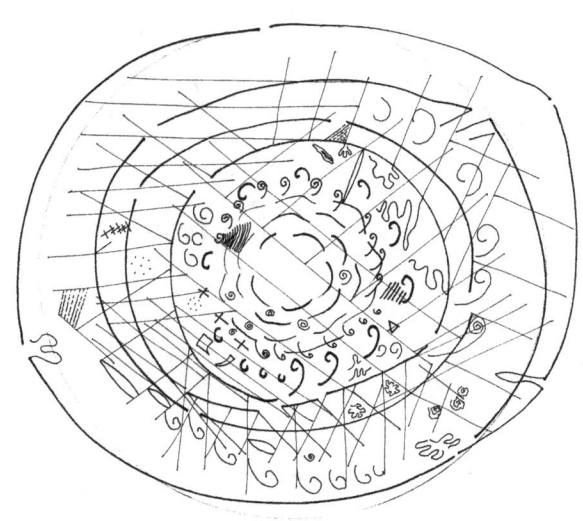

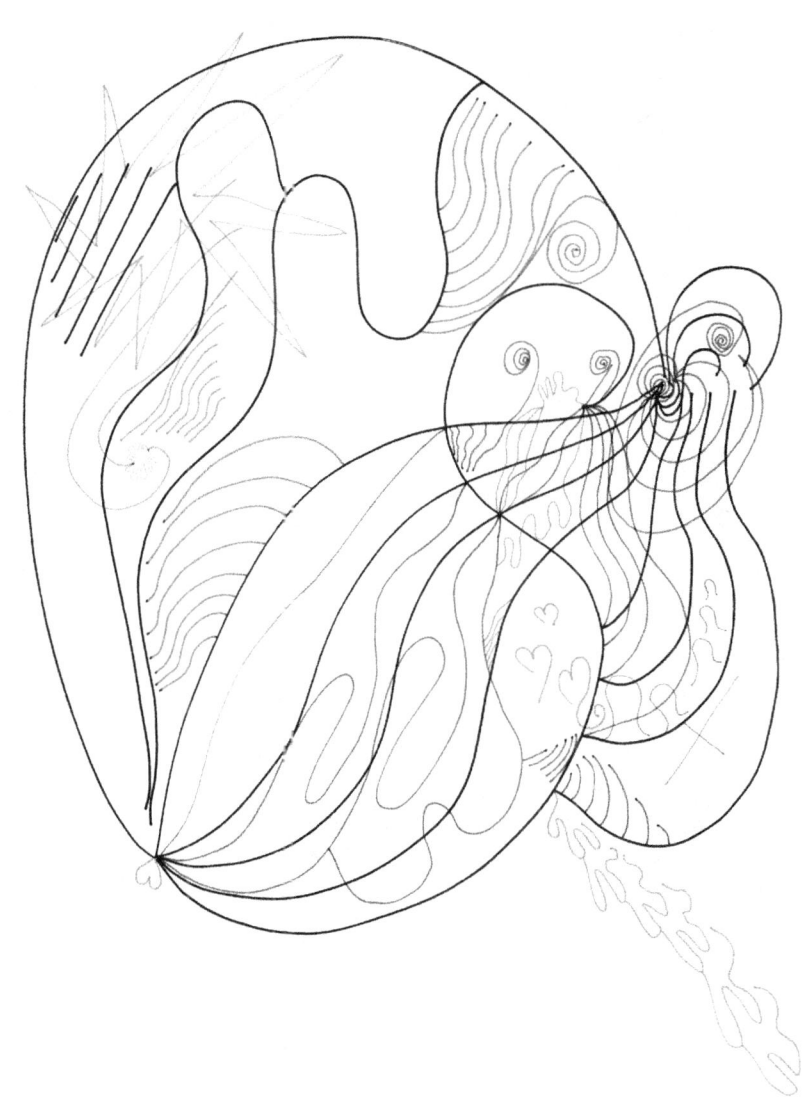

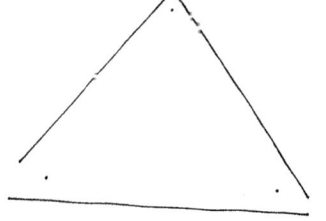

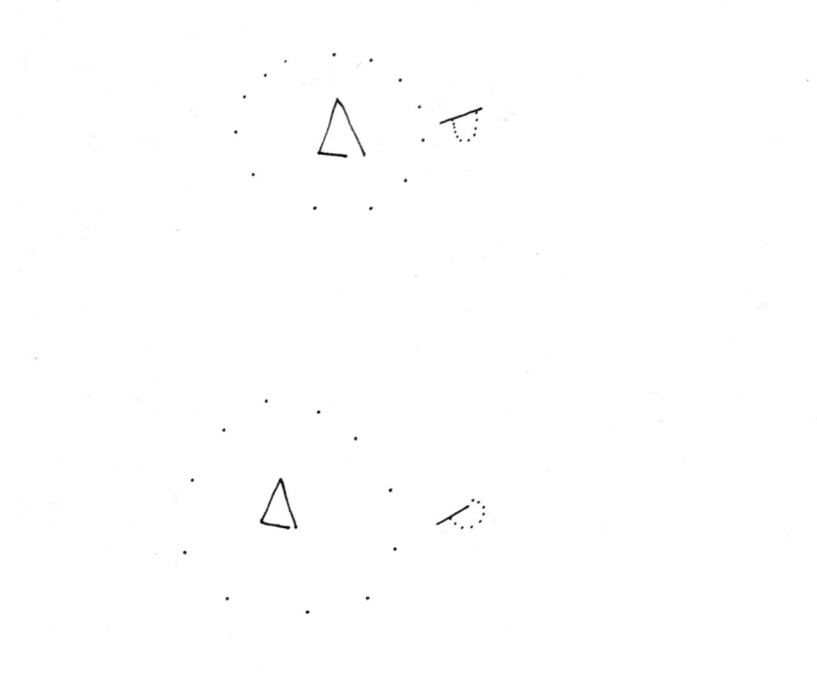

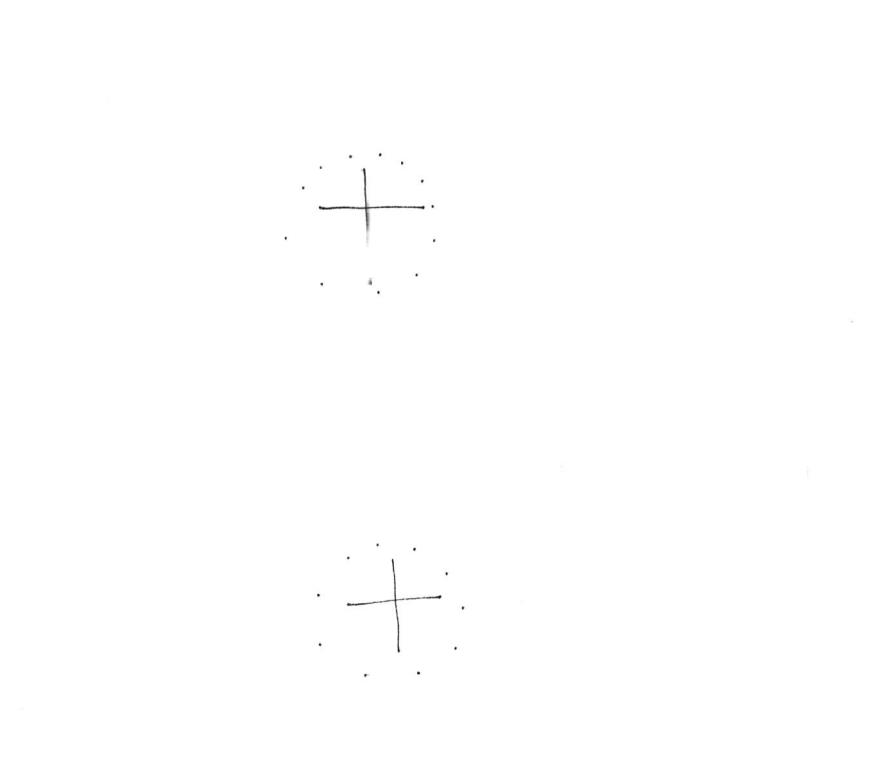

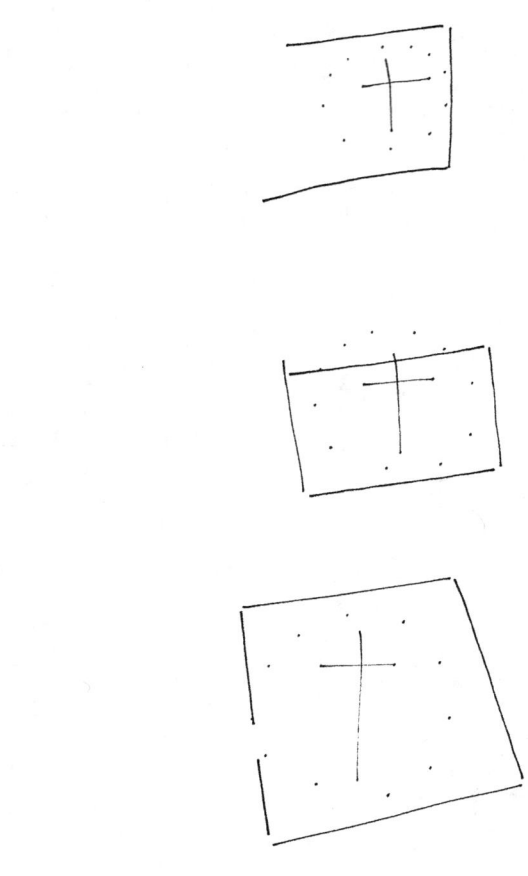

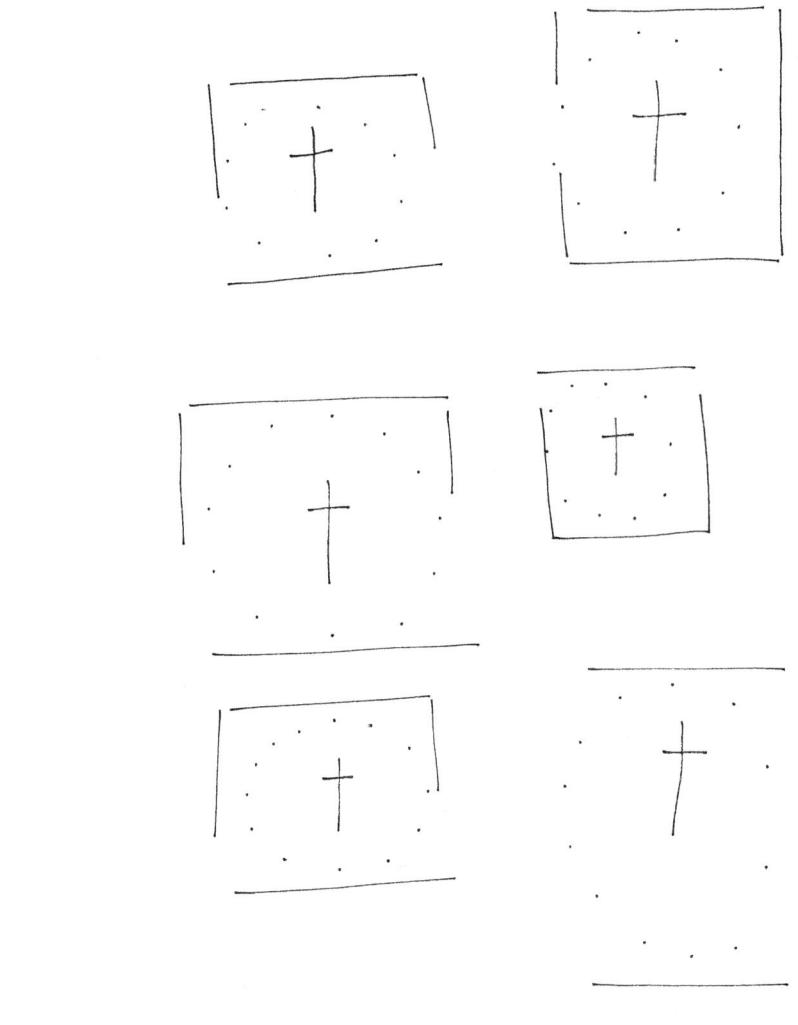

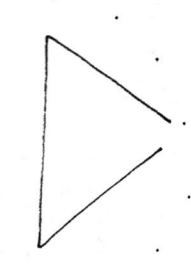

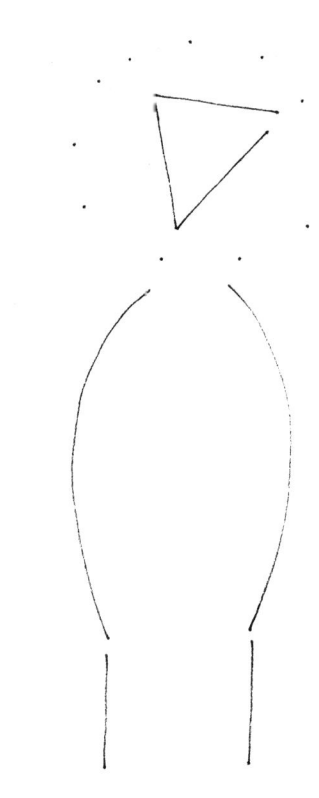

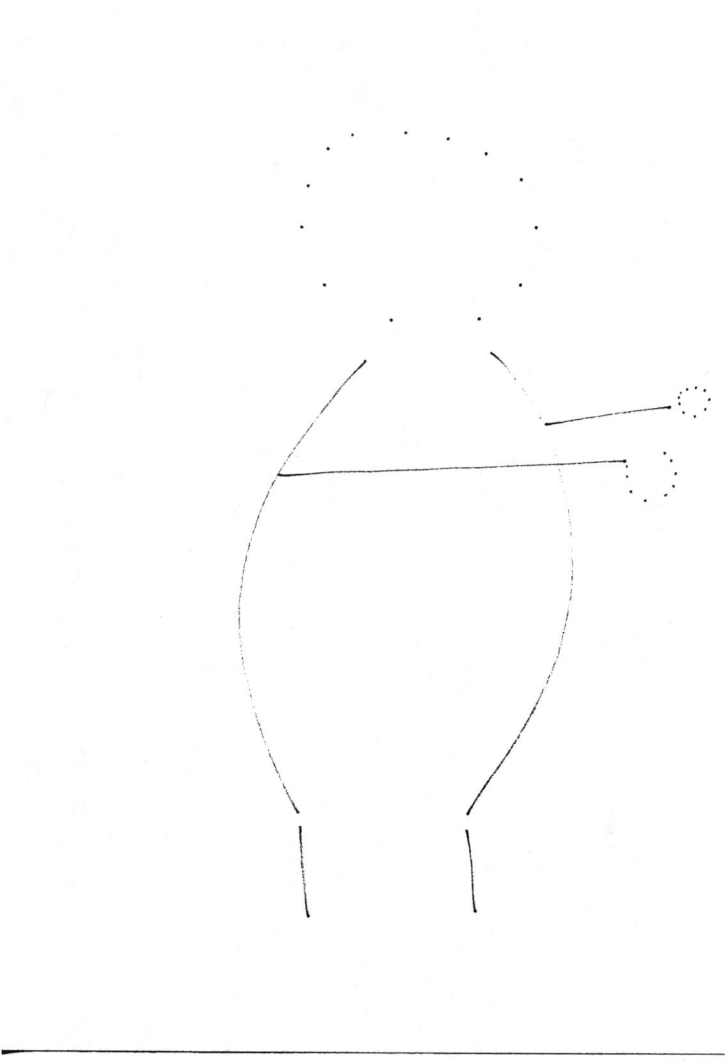

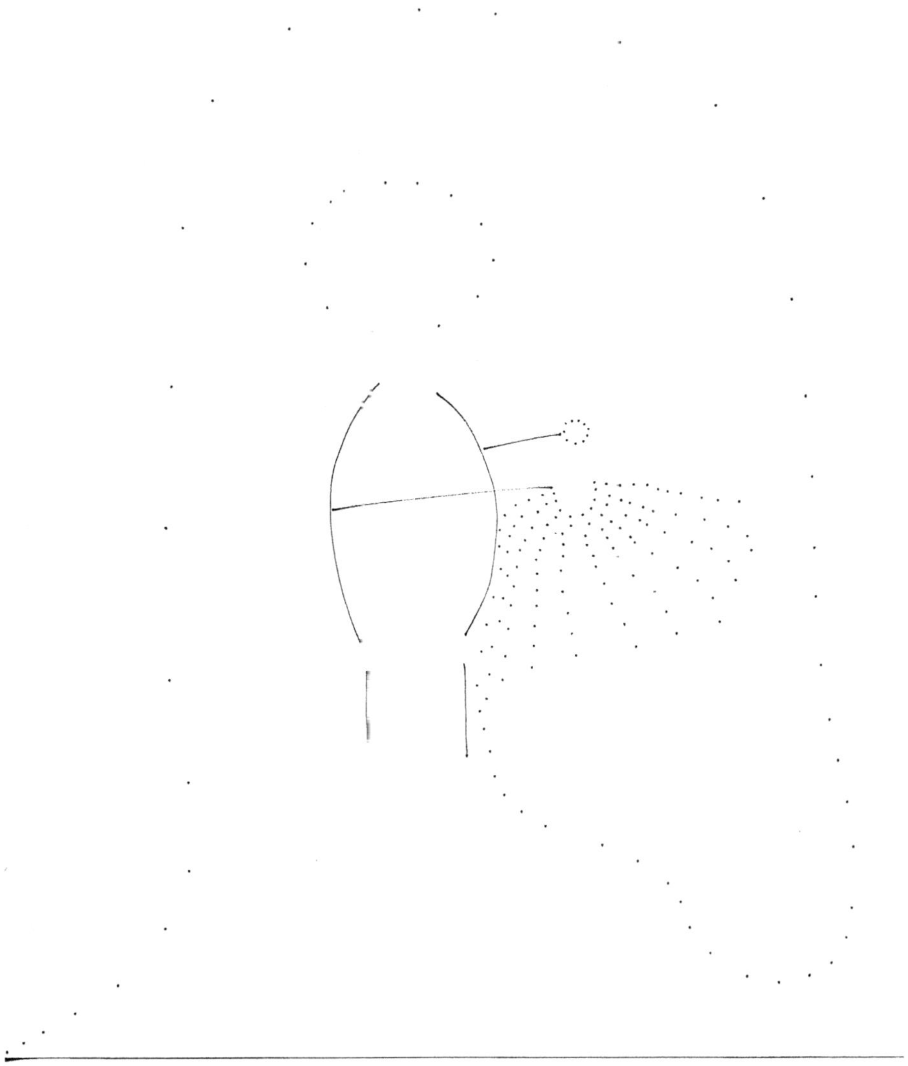

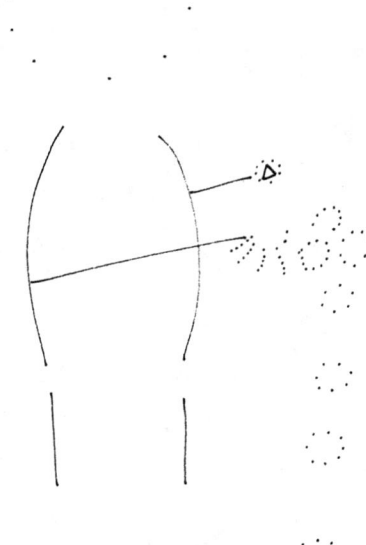

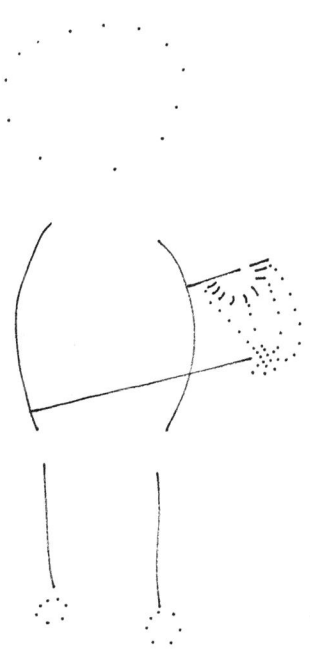

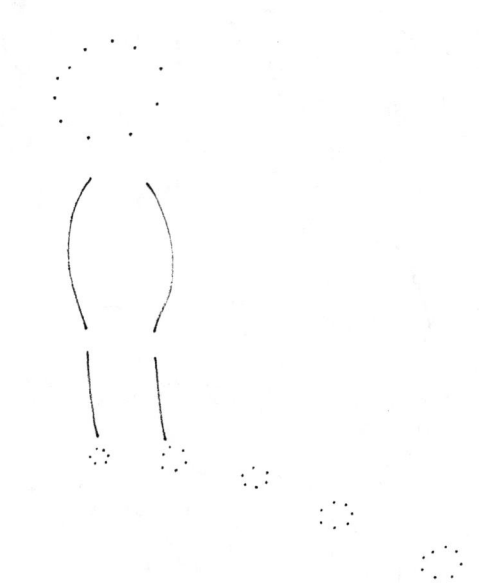

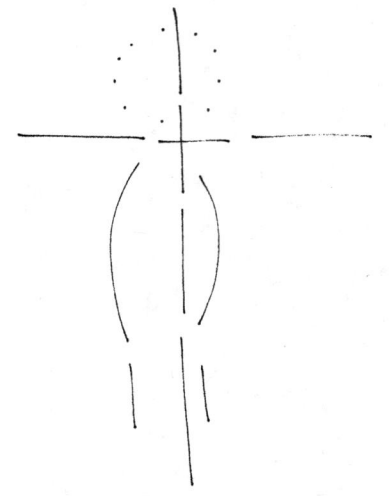

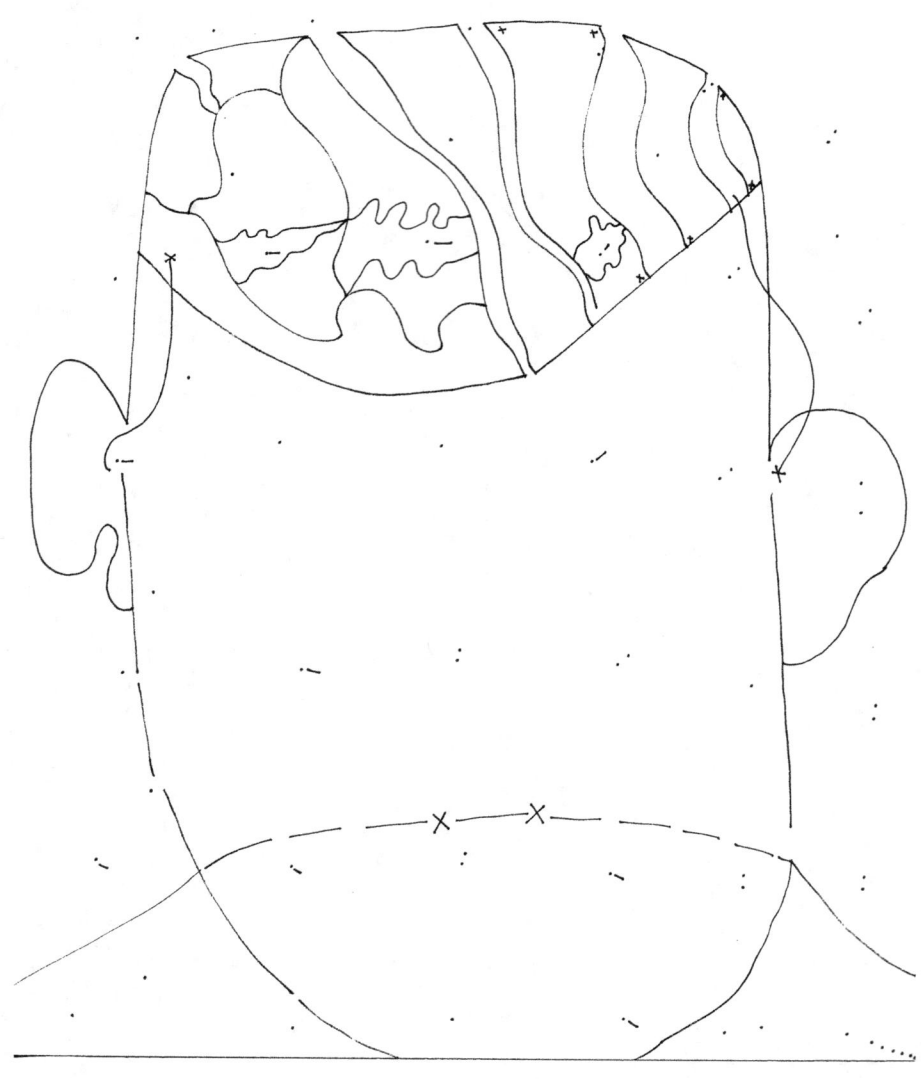

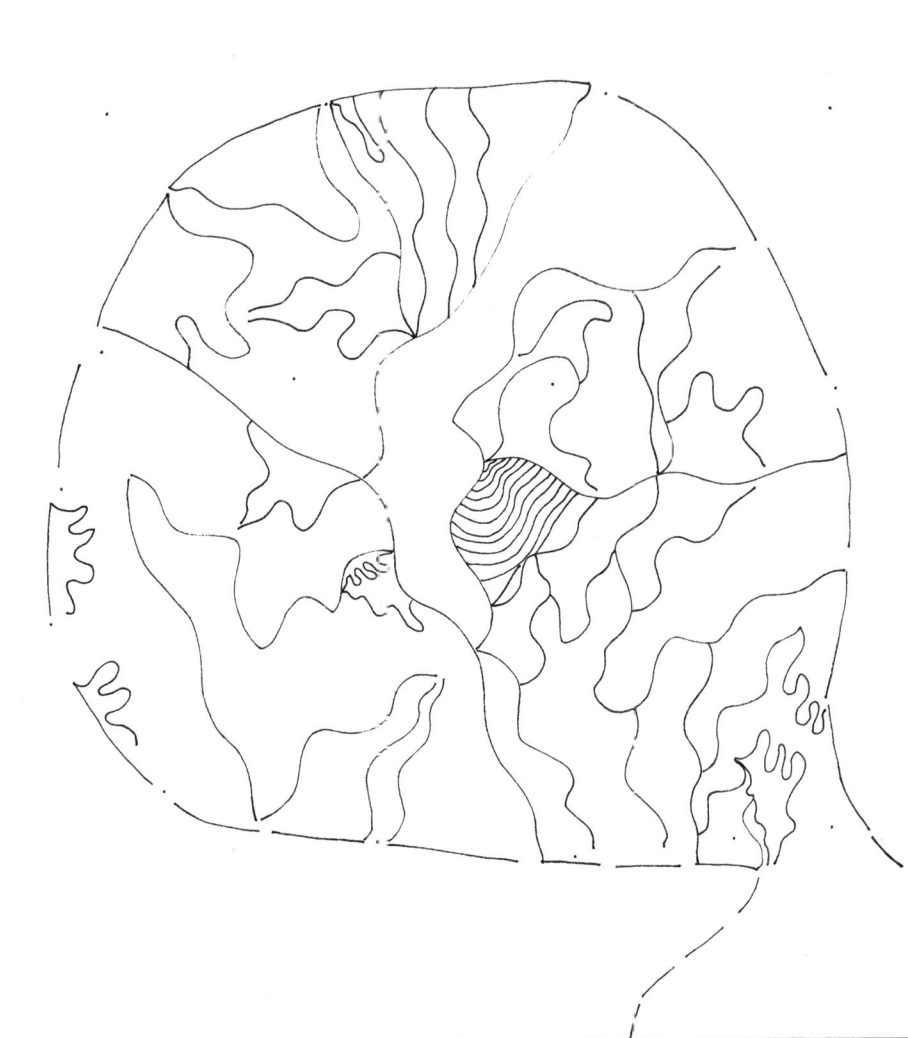

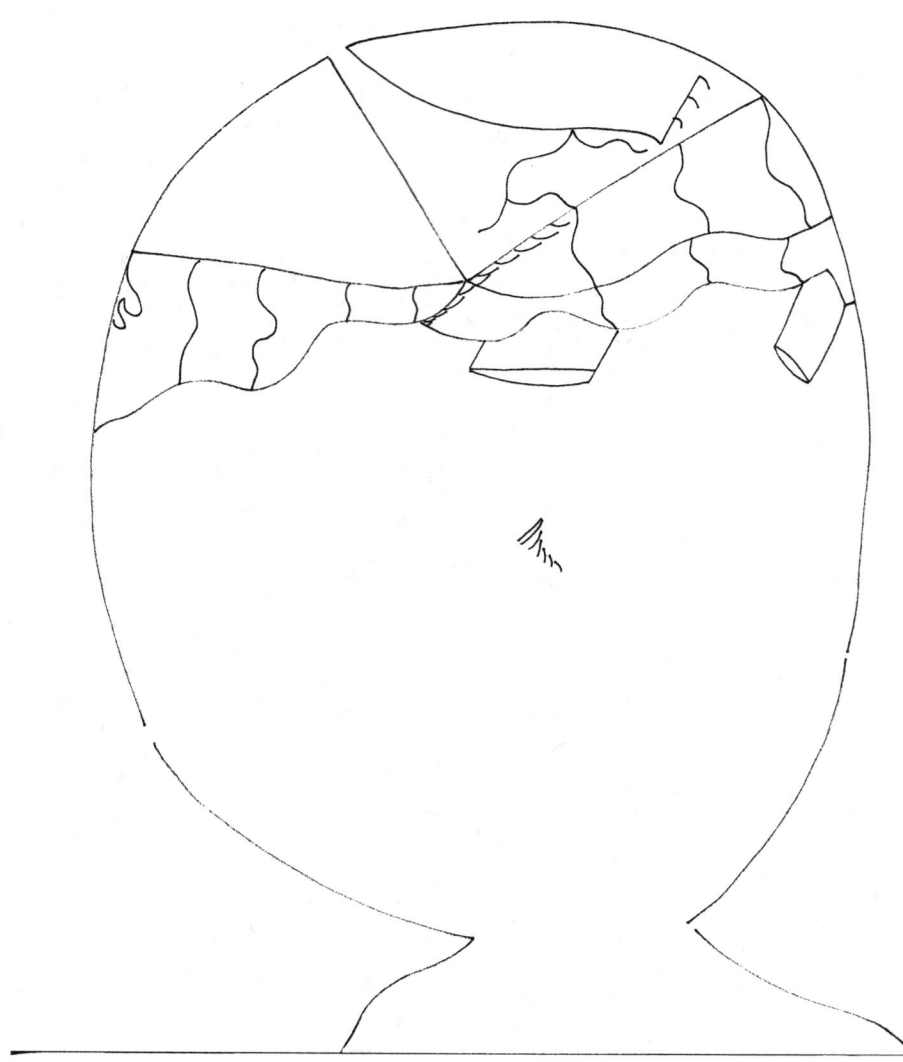

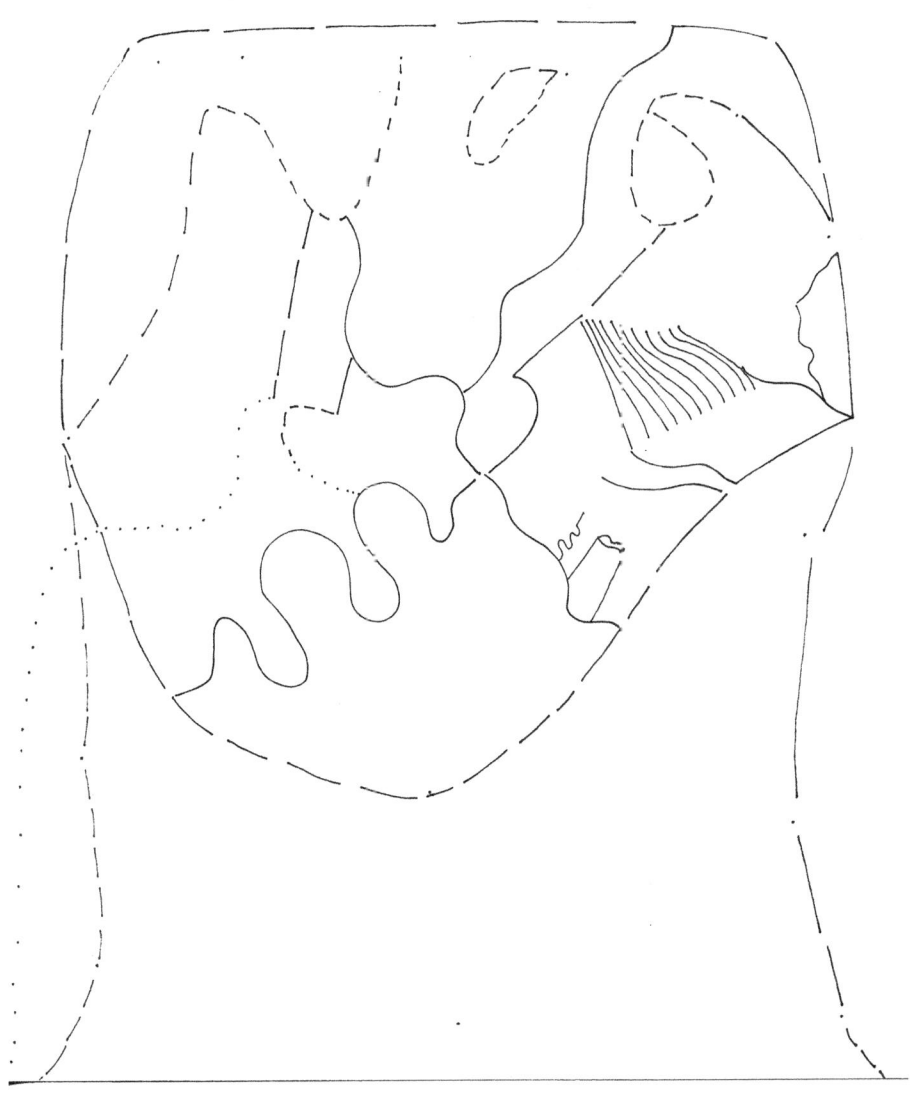

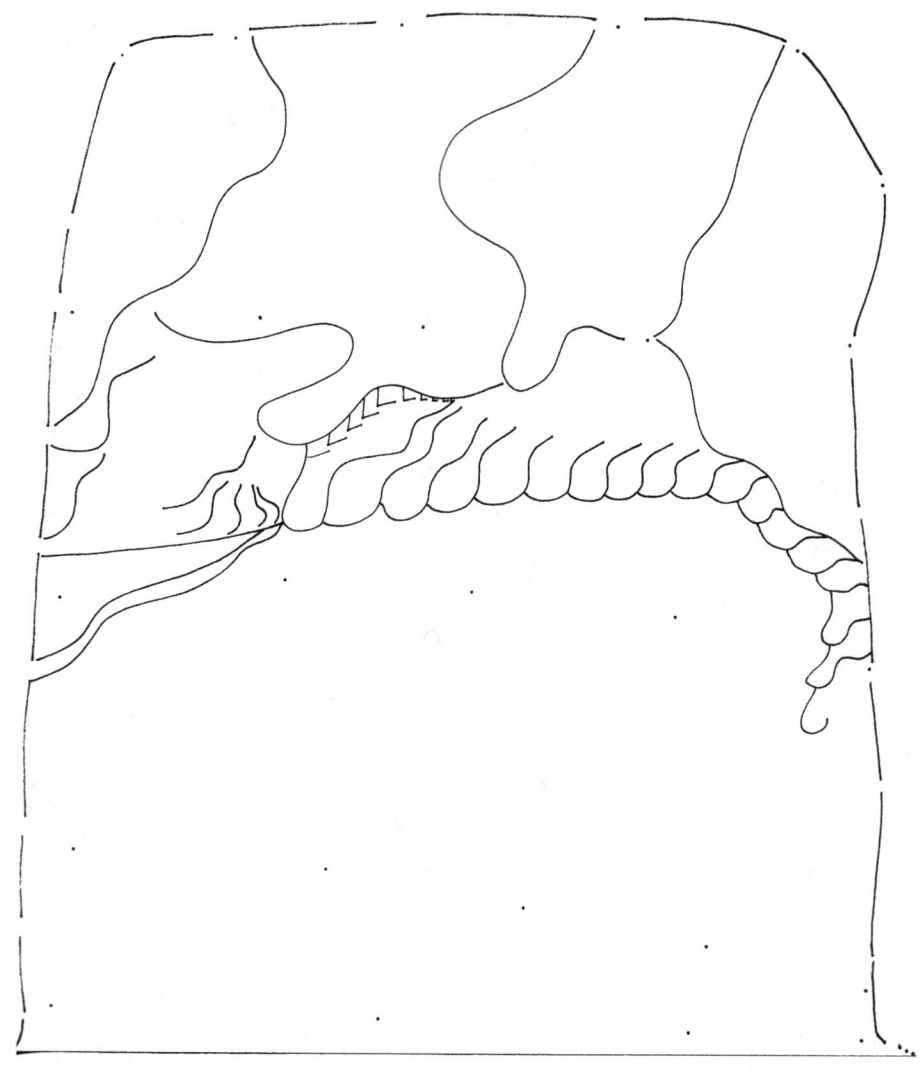

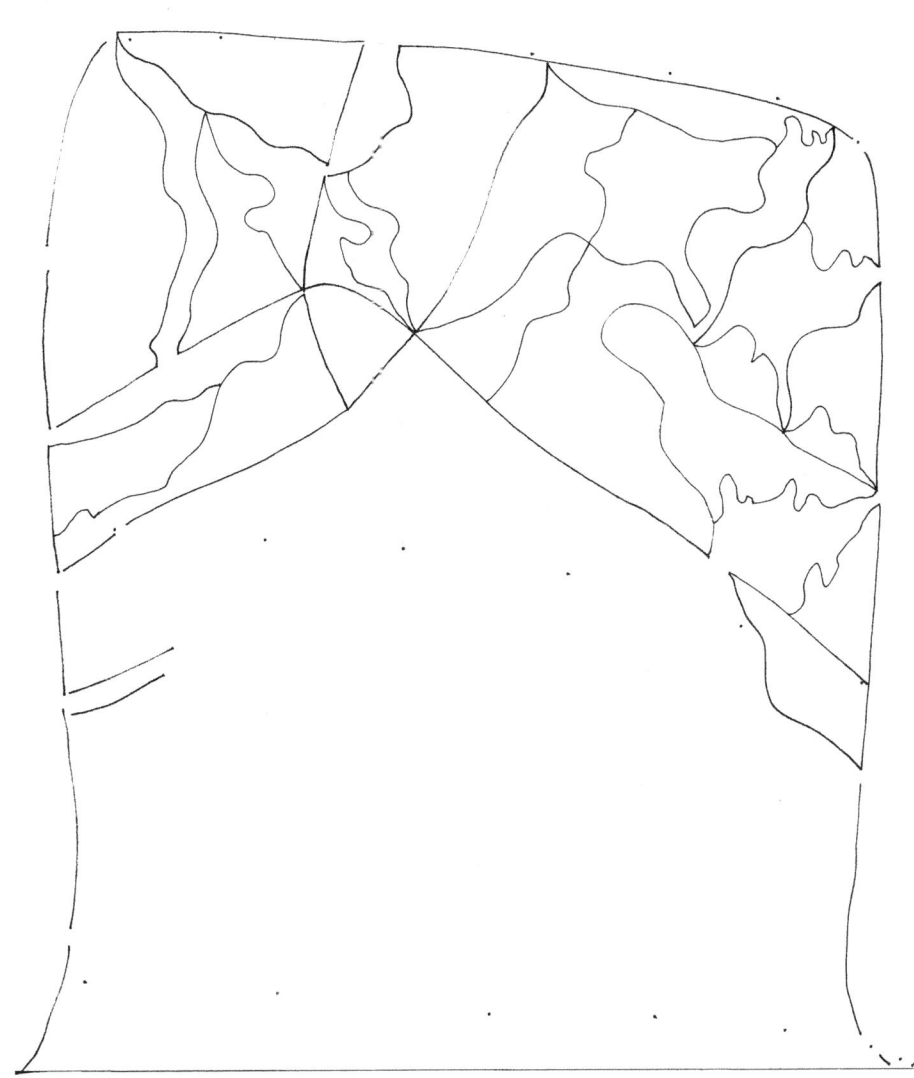

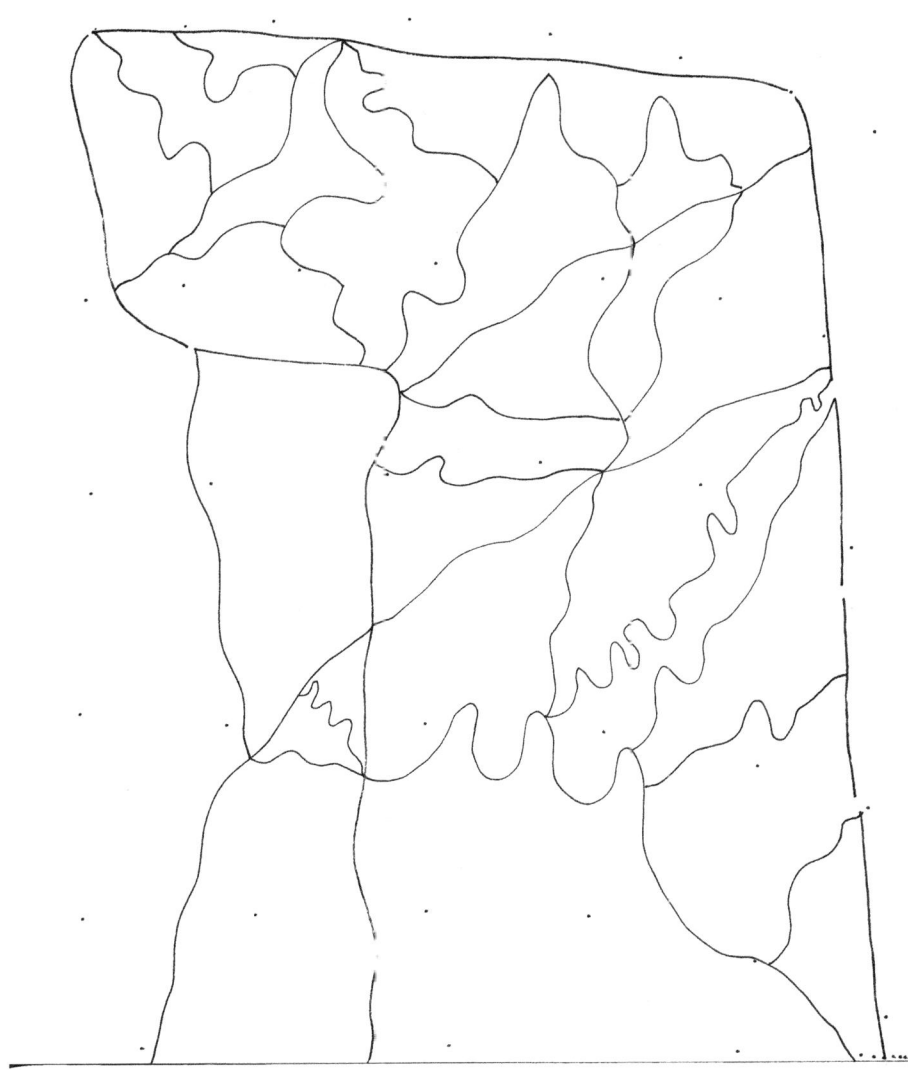

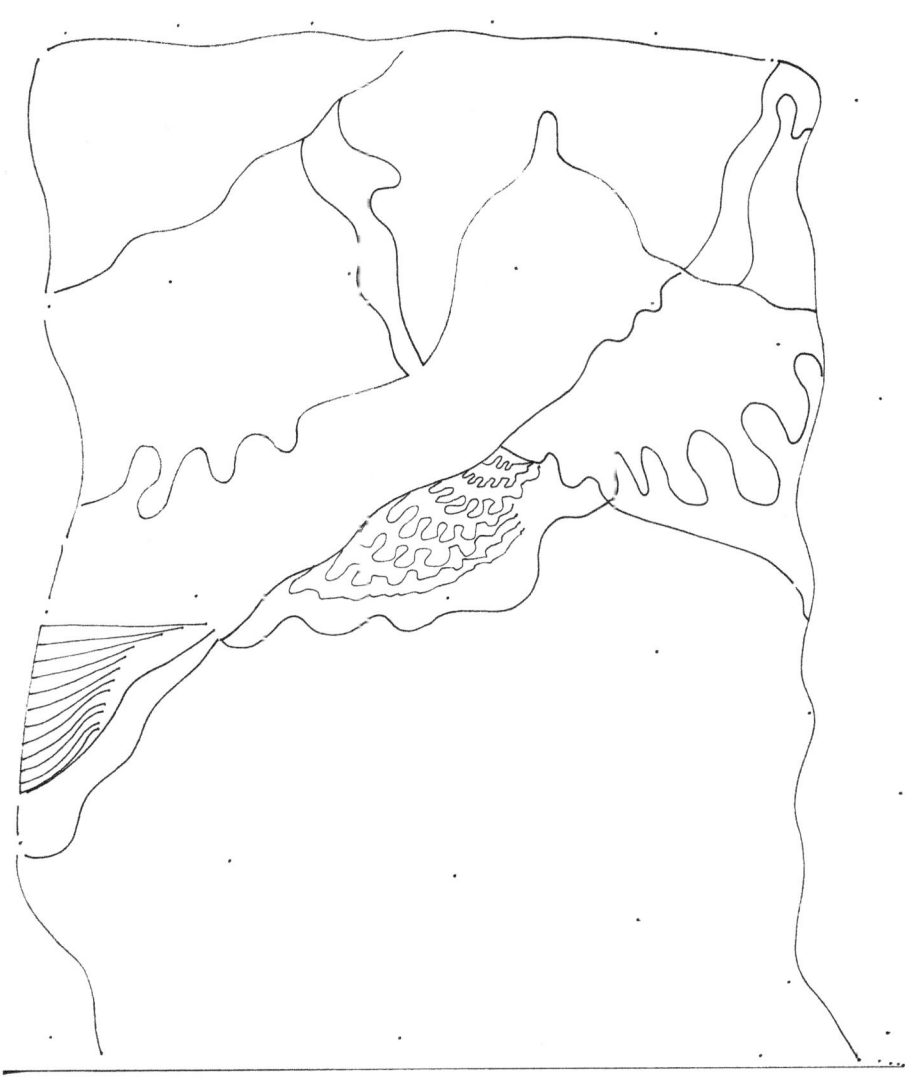

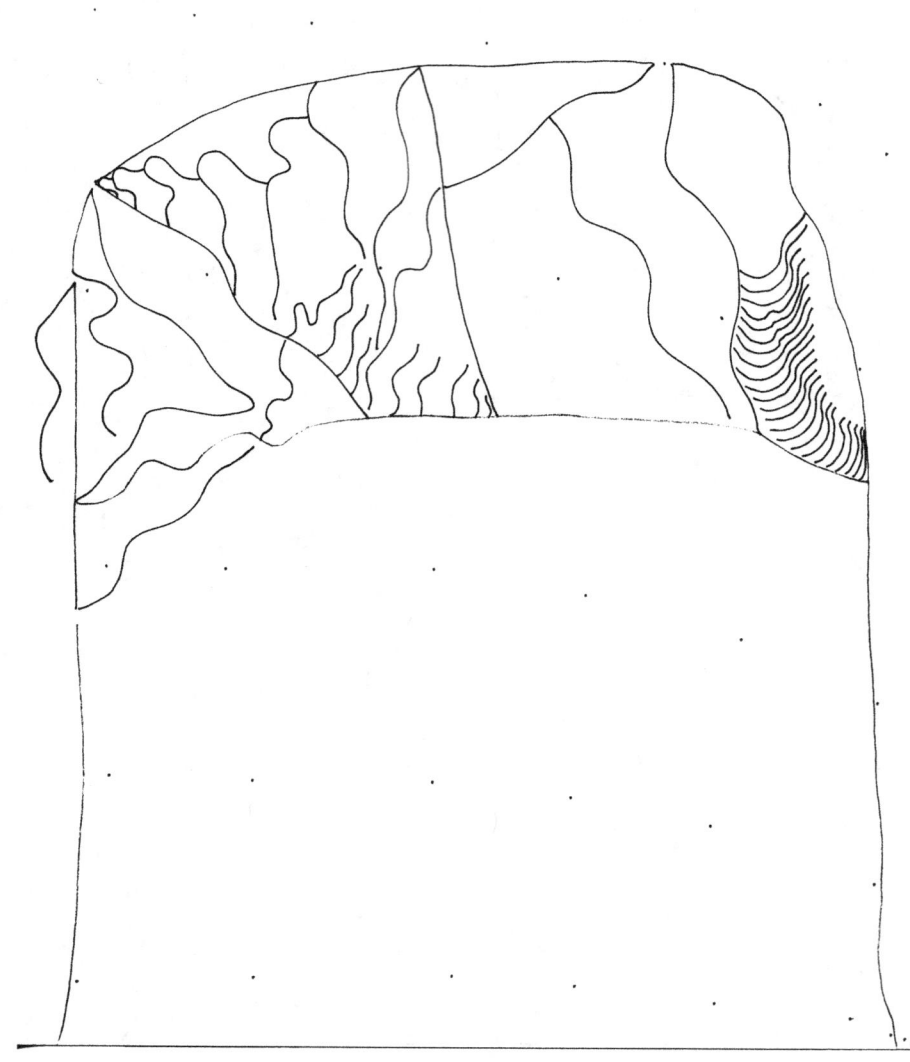

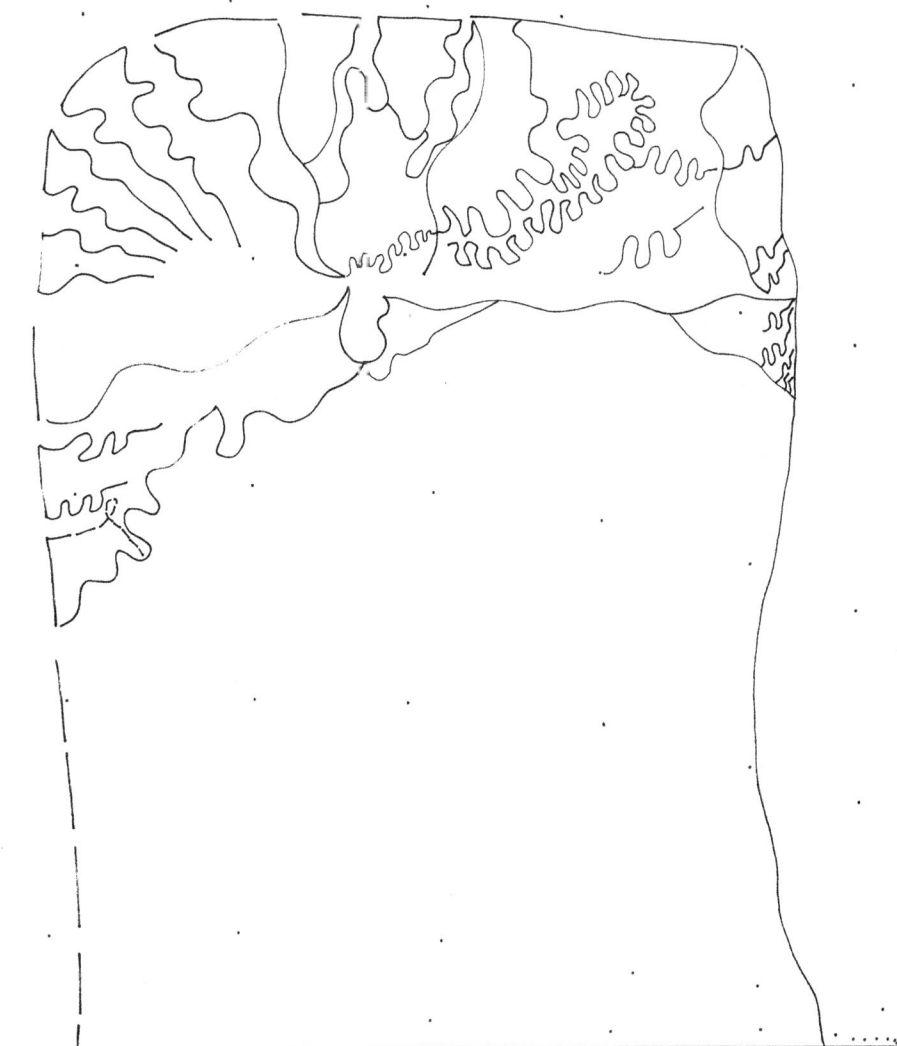

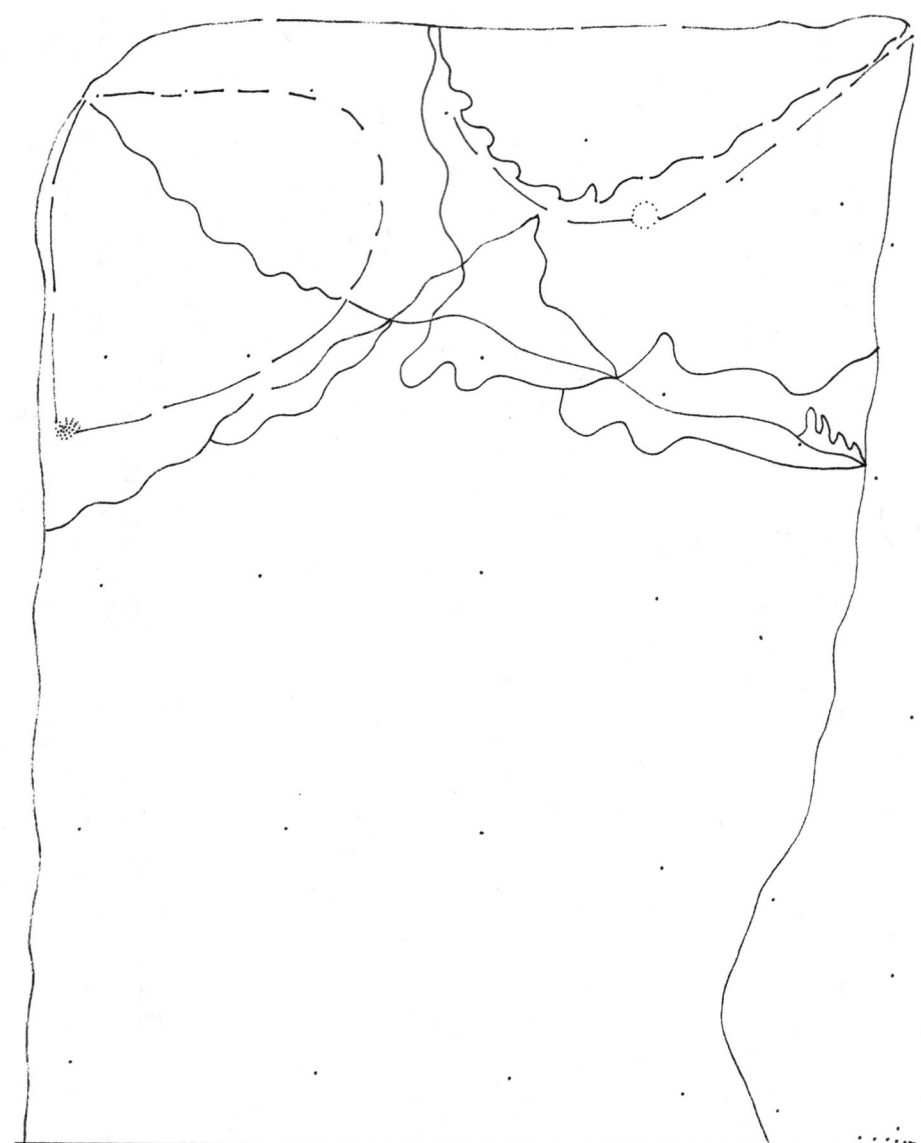

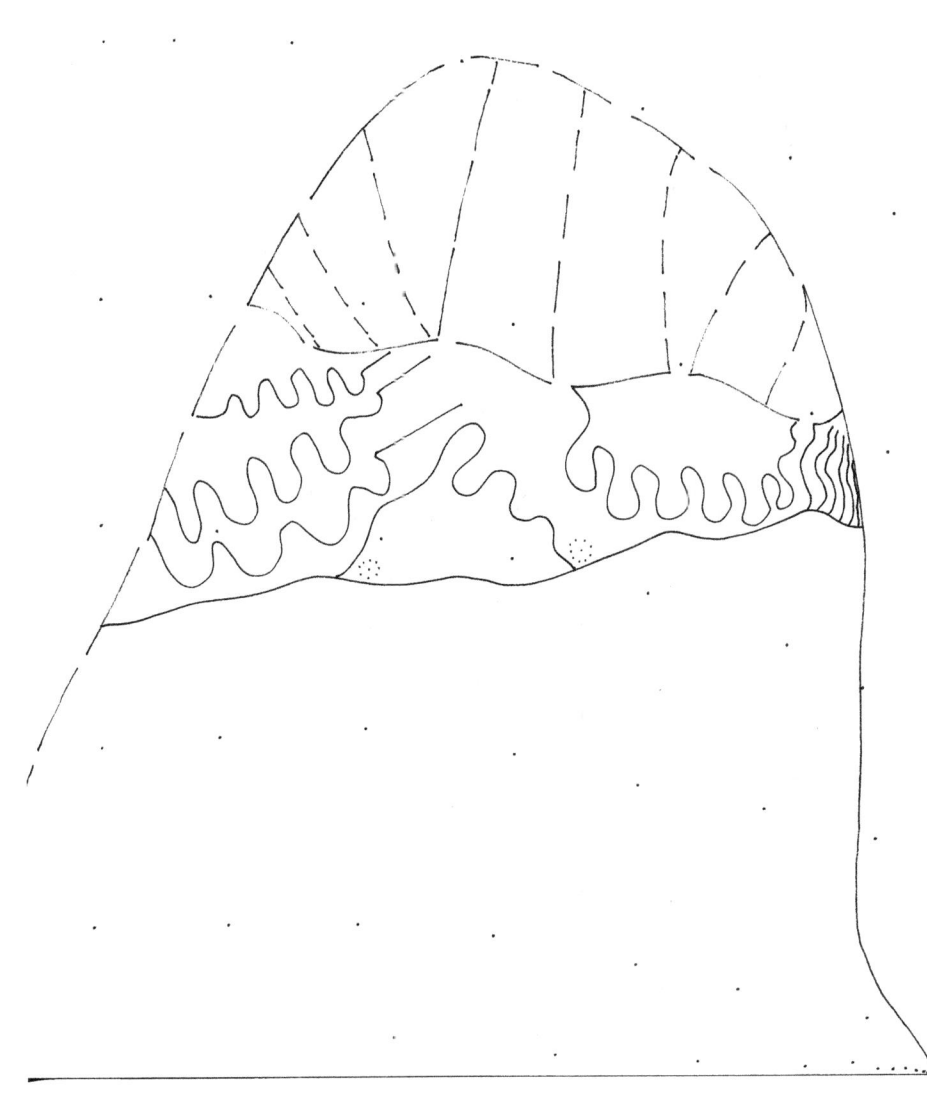

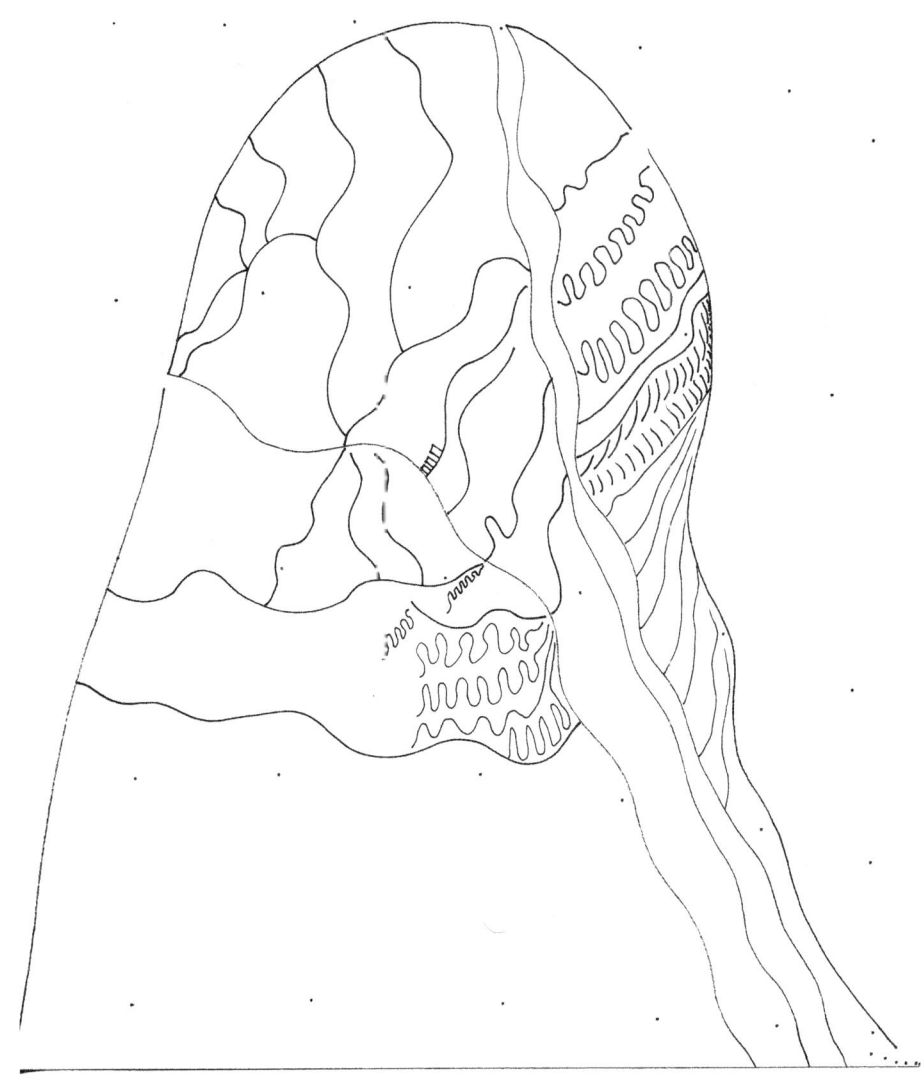

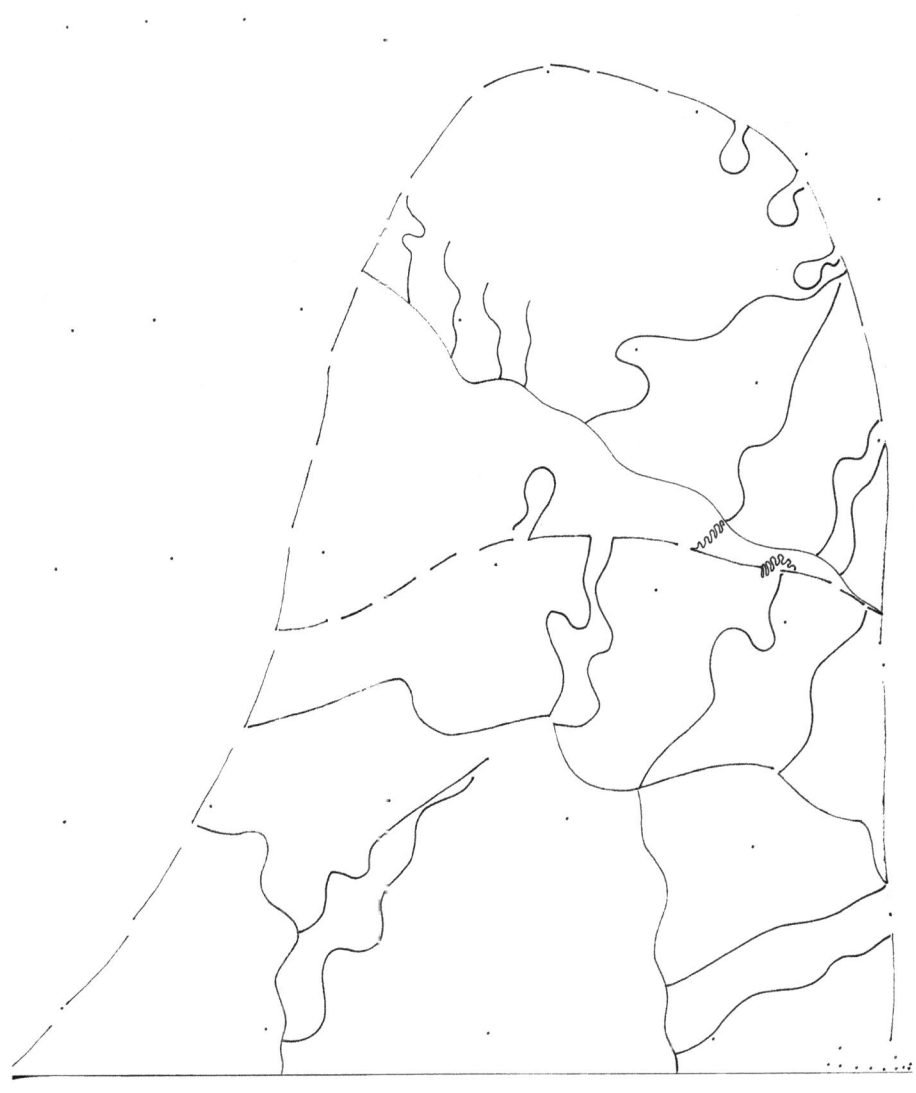

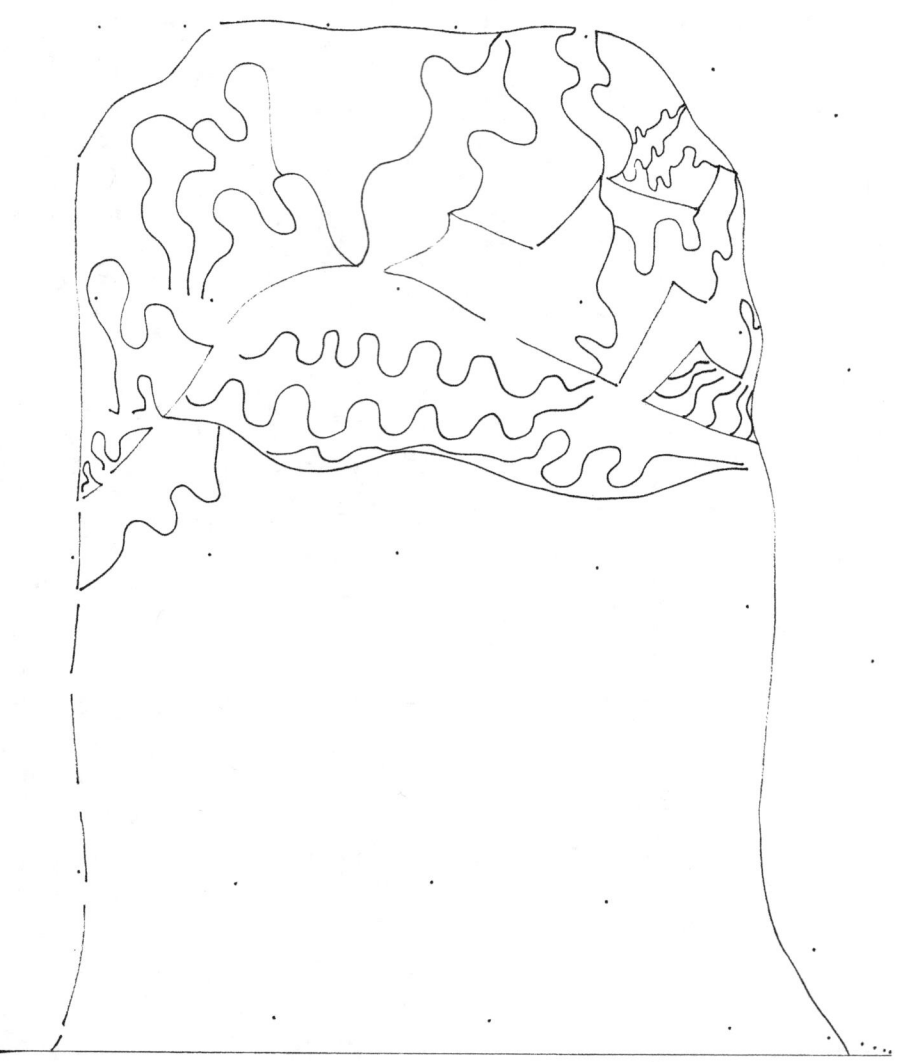

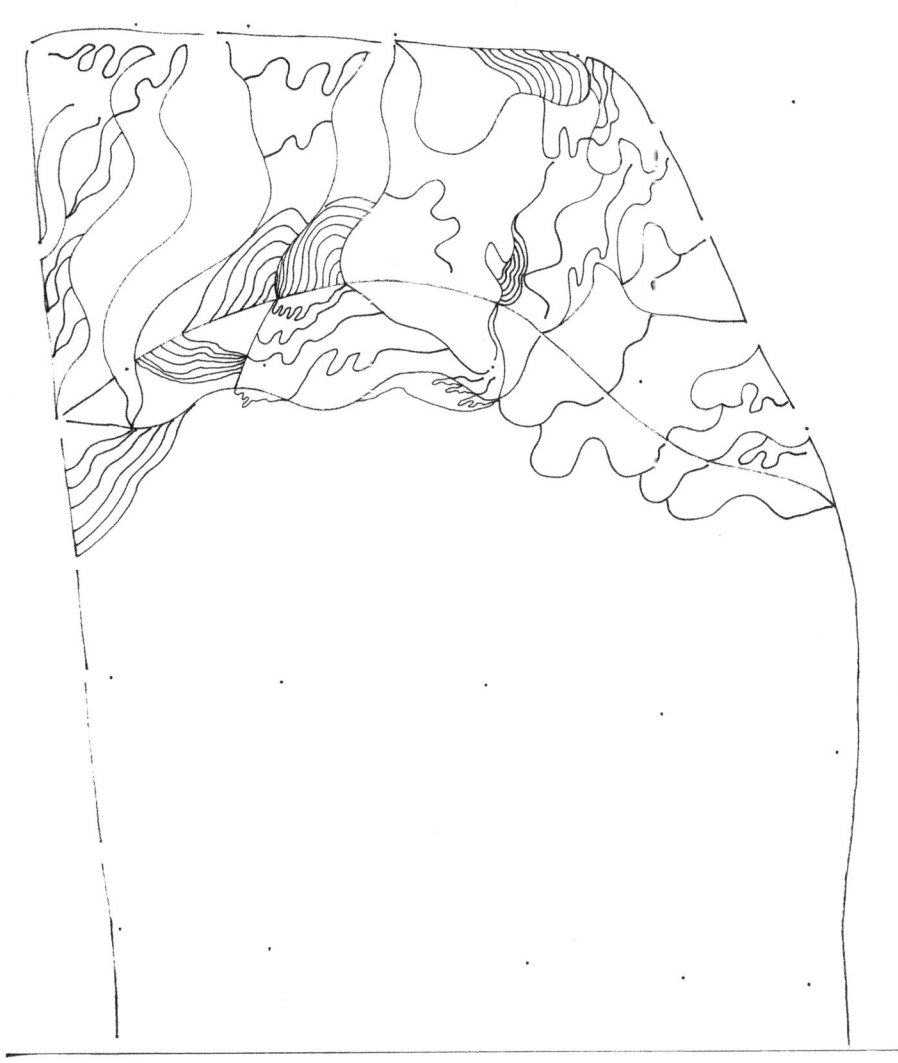

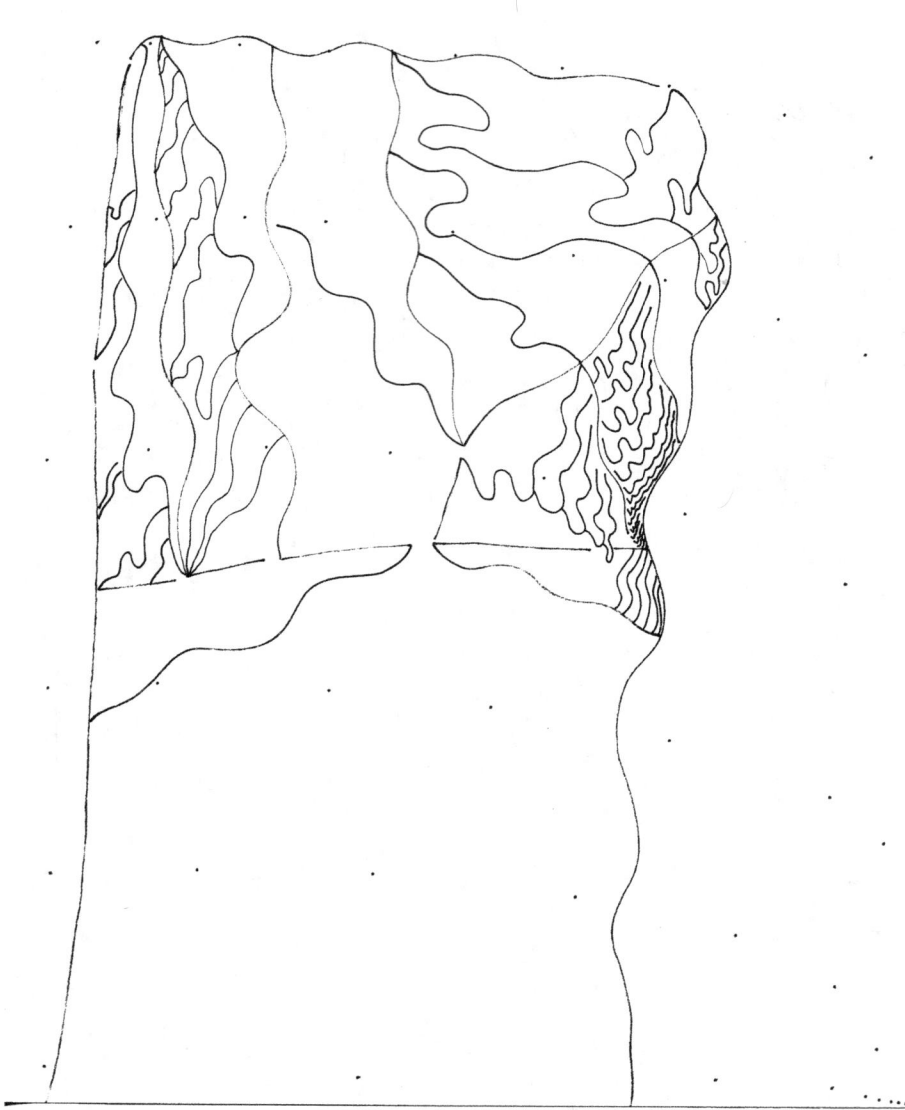

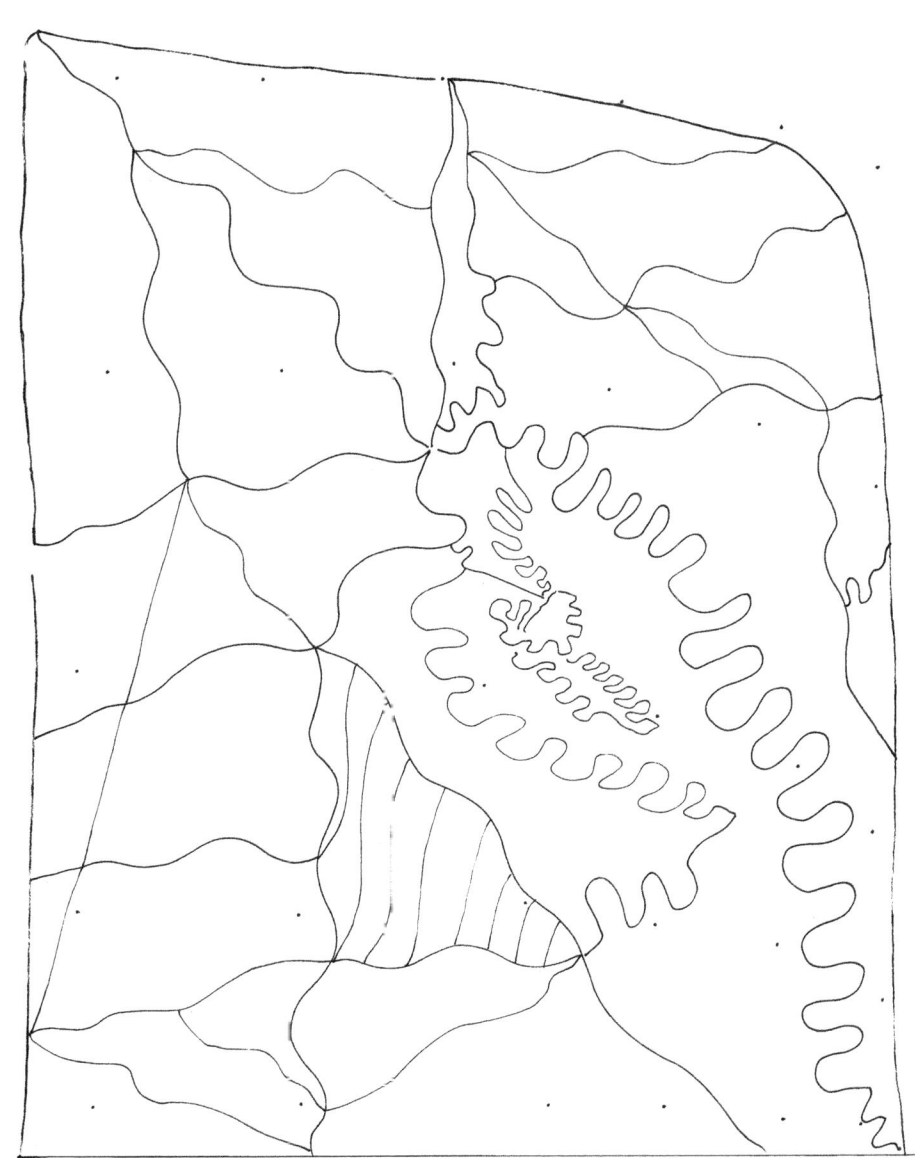

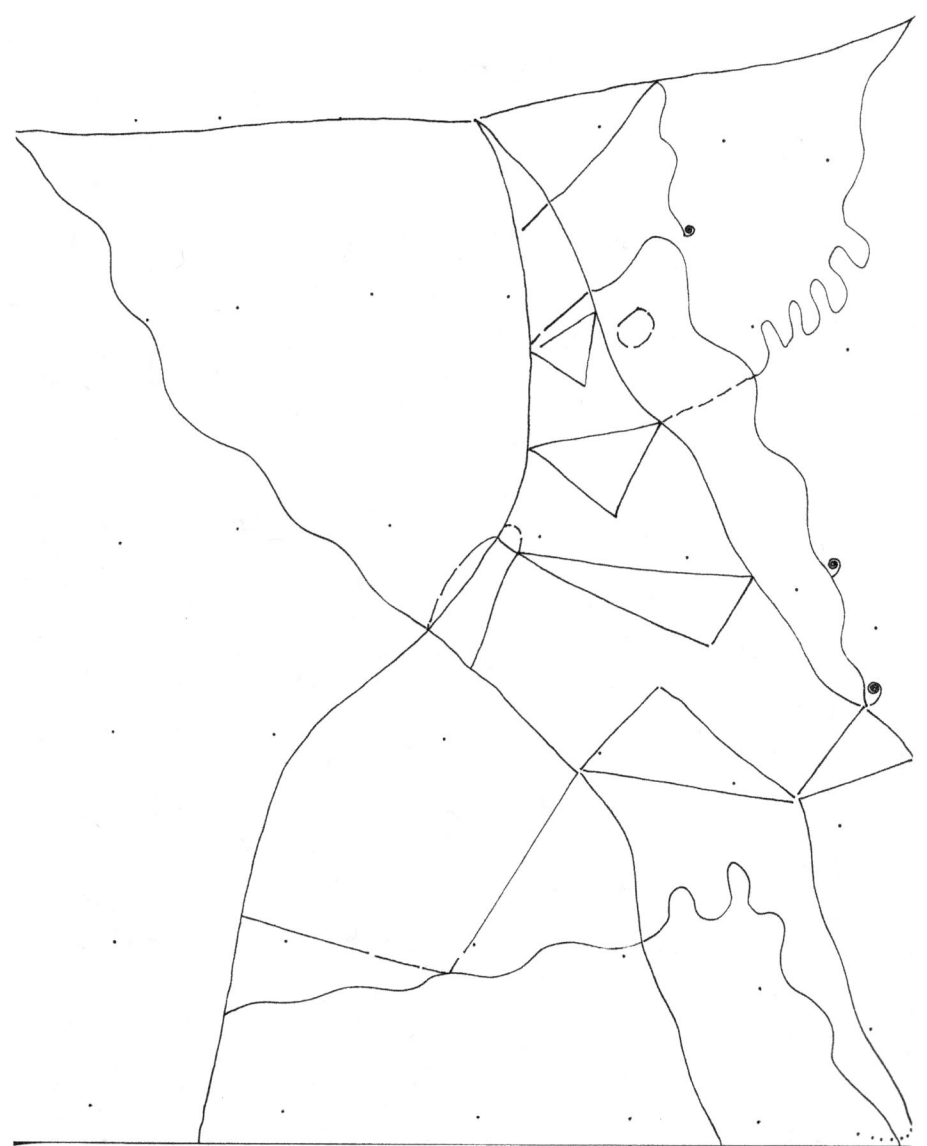

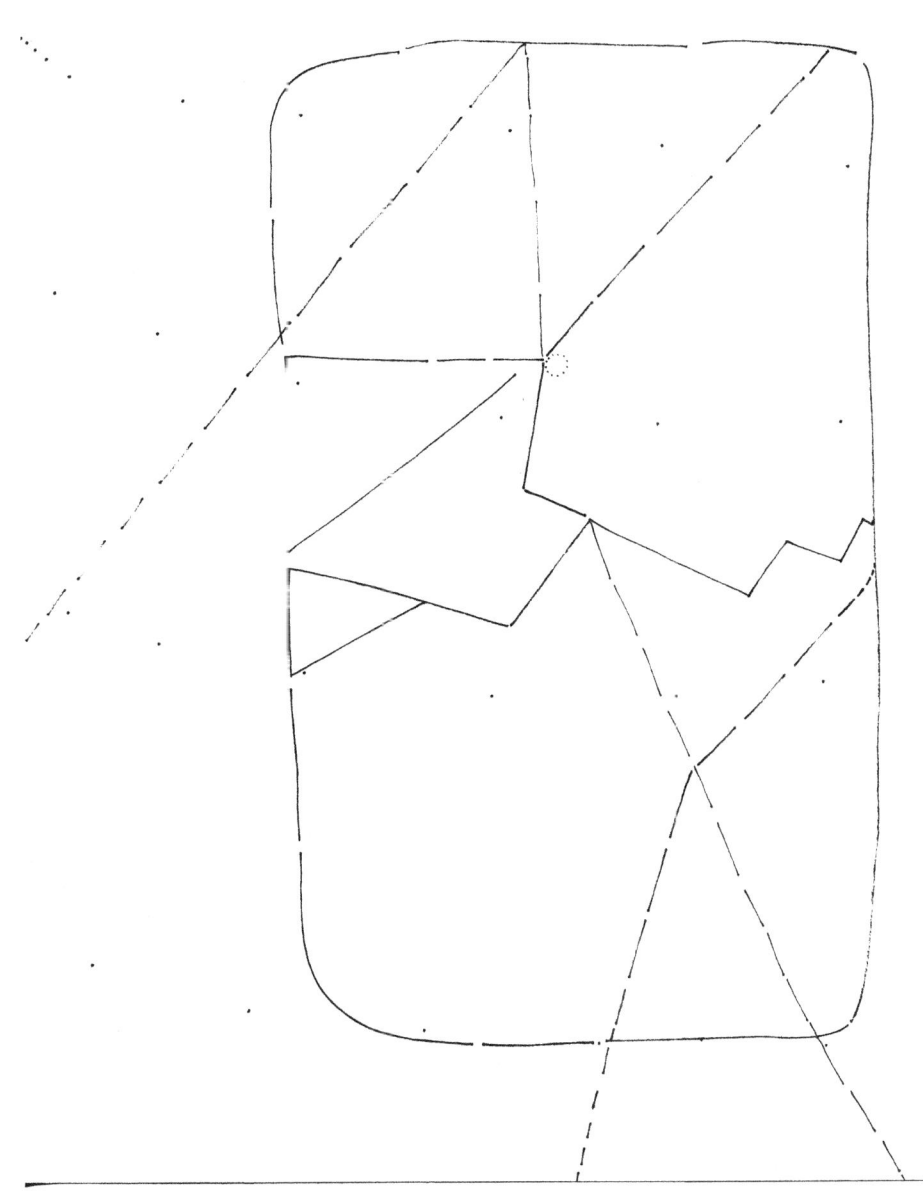

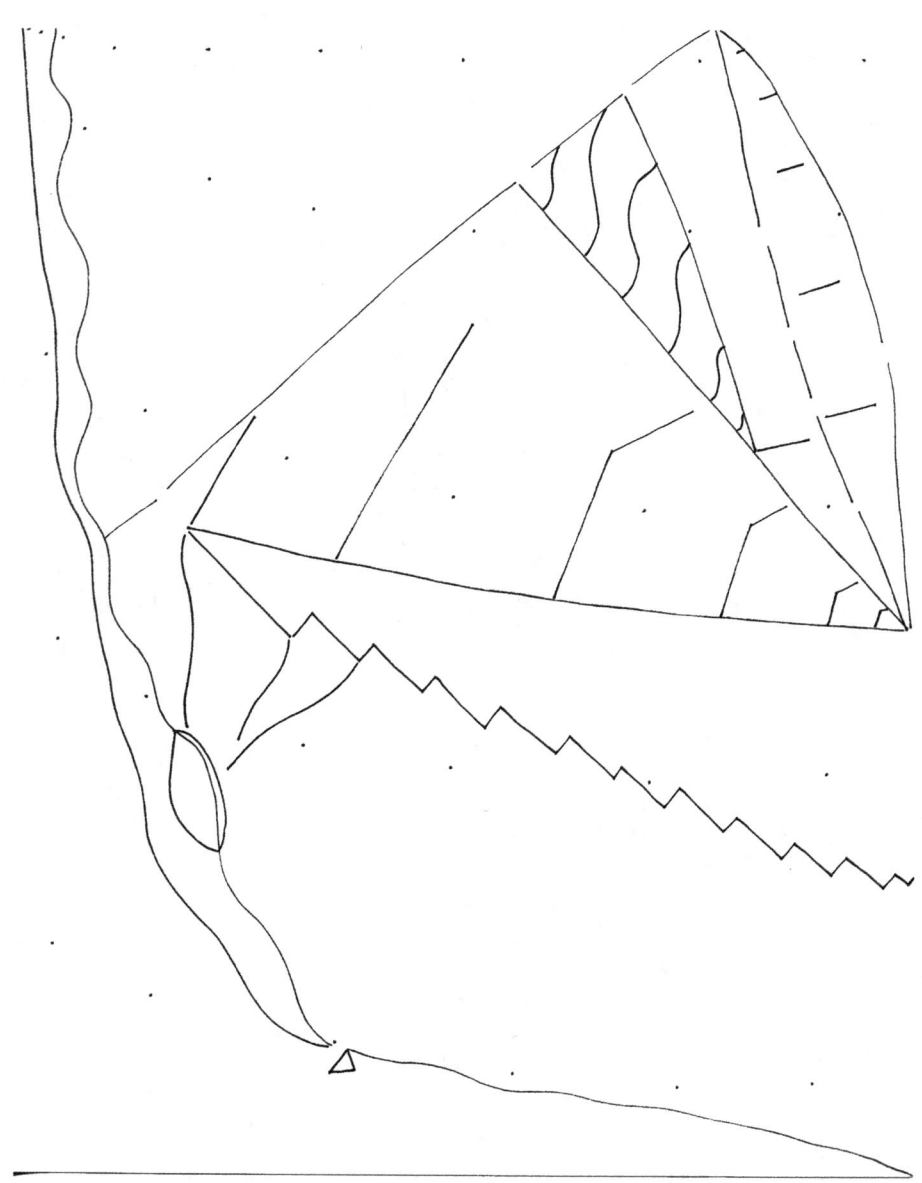

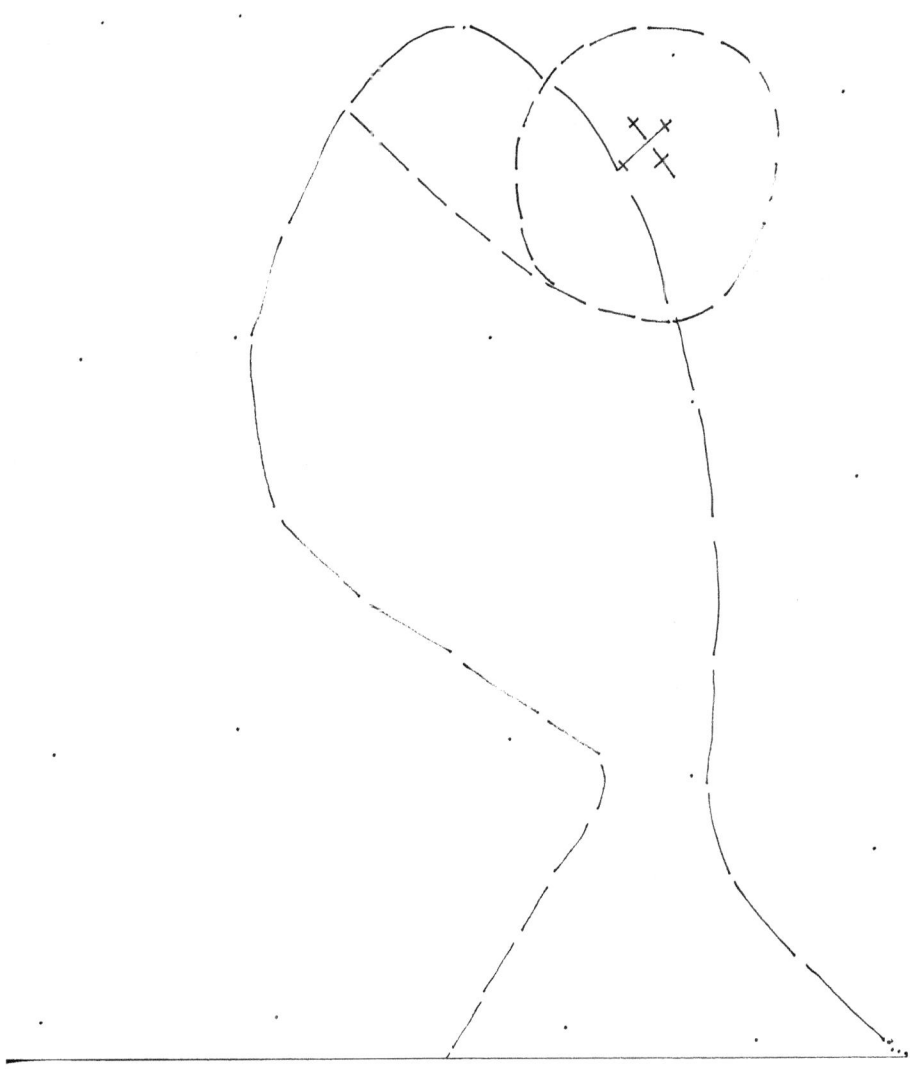

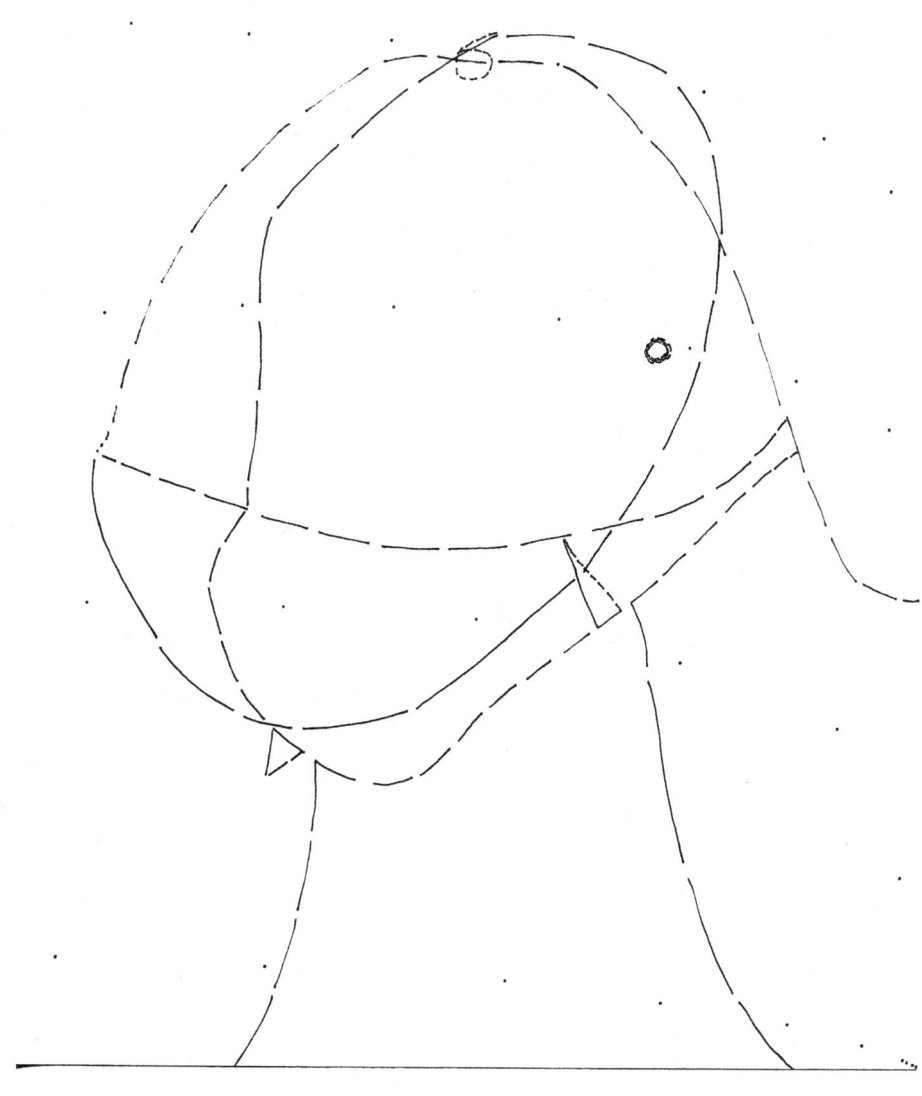

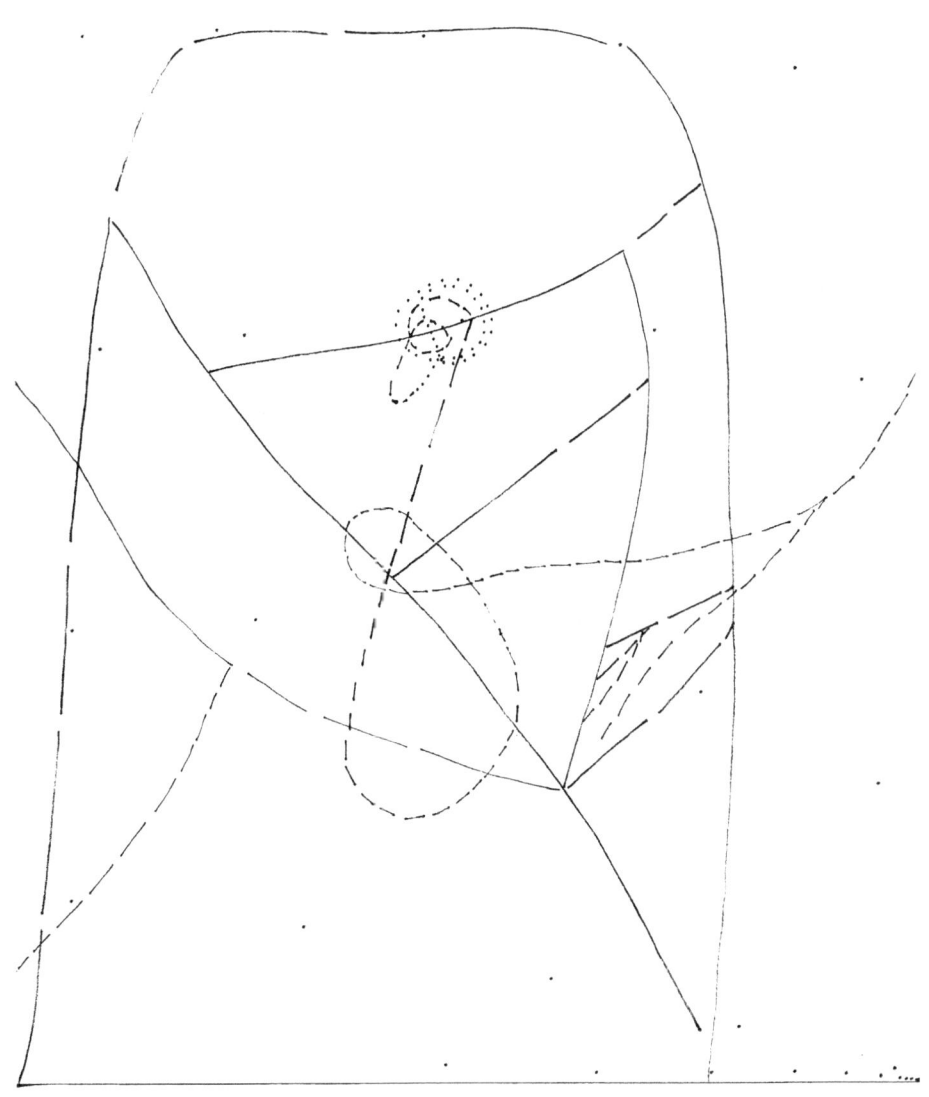